Empathy:
I Know How You Feel!

by Liz George

Content Consultant
Samantha Gambino, Psy.D.
Licensed Psychologist, New York, New York

Reading Consultant
Jeanne M. Clidas, Ph.D.
Reading Specialist

Children's Press®
An Imprint of Scholastic Inc.

A CIP catalog record of this book is available from the Library of Congress
ISBN 978-0-531-21512-8 (library binding) – ISBN 978-0-531-21380-3 (pbk.)

Produced by Spooky Cheetah Press
Design by Keith Plechaty

© 2016 by Scholastic Inc.

Printed in China 62

SCHOLASTIC, CHILDREN'S PRESS, ROOKIE TALK ABOUT IT™, and associated logos are trademarks and/or registered trademarks of Scholastic Inc.

1 2 3 4 5 6 7 8 9 10 R 25 24 23 22 21 20 19 18 17 16

Photographs ©: cover: Kevin Dodge/Media Bakery; 3 left: Kevin Dodge/Media Bakery; 3 right: Ron Chapple/Dreamstime; 4: Ken Karp Photography; 7: Kevin Dodge/Media Bakery; 8 top left: geotrac/iStockphoto; 8 top right: Belinda Pretorius/Shutterstock, Inc.; 8 bottom left: Alexandre Zveiger/Dreamstime; 8 bottom right: Bigandt_Photography/iStockphoto; 11: Fotografie Seckinger/Media Bakery; 12: Media Bakery; 15: rosliothman/iStockphoto; 16: Oliver Rossi/Media Bakery; 19: Ron Chapple/Dreamstime; 20: Blend Images/Superstock, Inc.; 23: Media Bakery; 24: SW Productions/Media Bakery; 26 bottom: Mohit Gupta/Yash Gupta; 26 top: Norman Chan/Shutterstock, Inc.; 27 bottom: Courtesy CNN/Yash Gupta; 27 top: paulista/Shutterstock, Inc.; 28: ArtisticCaptures/iStockphoto; 29: Janet Kimber/Media Bakery; 30: SW Productions/Media Bakery; 31 top: geotrac/iStockphoto; 31 center top: Ron Chapple/Dreamstime; 31 center bottom: Media Bakery; 31 bottom: Oliver Rossi/Media Bakery.

Table of Contents

What Is Empathy?

Your friend looks sad. She drew a picture and it got ripped. You say, "I am sorry. I know how that feels." You are showing **empathy**!

Empathy is understanding your friend's feelings and caring about them. You can **imagine** how he or she feels. That lets you share the same **emotion**.

happy

sad

angry

surprised

8

You Get Me!

Can you name some emotions? How about happiness, sadness, or anger?

Everyone feels emotions. It is important to know our own emotions. That helps us see how others feel, too.

"Try walking in someone else's shoes." Have you ever heard anyone say that? It means that you should try to imagine how someone else feels.

When you walk in someone else's shoes, you feel what they feel. And you can feel empathy for the other person.

Walking in someone else's shoes does not really mean you put on someone else's shoes!

11

Here are some ways to have and show empathy:

- Remember or imagine how you would feel in another person's shoes.

- Watch and listen closely to what another person is doing or saying.

- Ask what another person is feeling.

- Let the person know you understand and care about how he or she is feeling.

Showing You Care

Some kids are great at showing empathy. You have probably been in the same **situations** they have. When you read the stories about these kids, ask yourself, "What would I do?"

Anna is upset. She lost her favorite eraser. It had sparkles on it.

Molly remembers when she lost her favorite pencil. It smelled like cupcakes. She remembers how upset she was. She knows just how Anna feels. Molly says, "I am sorry you lost your eraser."

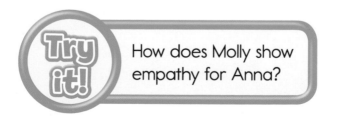

Try it!

How does Molly show empathy for Anna?

Jack watches his mother clean the kitchen while he eats his snack. He notices that she is not smiling like she usually does. She often sings while she cleans, too. But today his mom is quiet. She seems sad.

Jack thinks about what might cheer his mom up. He knows she loves his hugs. He hops off his chair and gives her a big squeeze. Now Mom has a big smile on her face!

Try it!

What clues told Jack his mom might need a hug?

Mason just started at Ben's school. Now he is sitting all alone at recess. Ben goes over and asks Mason how he is doing. "It is lonely to be in a new school with no friends," Mason says.

Ben imagines how he would feel in Mason's place. He asks him if he wants to play. They play together and have a great time!

Try it! How does Ben walk in Mason's shoes?

Some kids are whispering about Isabella. She thinks they are making fun of her. She looks like she will cry.

Ryan knows it does not feel good to be teased. He tells Isabella it has happened to him before—and it made him feel really sad. "I know what will help," he says. "Let's go sit somewhere else."

Try it! How does Ryan let Isabella know he cares?

Empathy Works Both Ways

Share your feelings. That lets your friends understand how you feel. Then they will know they can share with you, too.

When friends care about each other, everyone feels good!

Try it! Think of a time when someone noticed how you were feeling and asked you about it. How did that help you?

Yash Gupta

Teenager Yash Gupta provides eyeglasses to kids in need all around the world.

Yash started wearing glasses when he was five years old. When he accidentally broke his glasses in high school, Yash spent a week going to school without them. Everything was blurry. He had trouble seeing his teacher and the blackboard. Yash imagined how hard it must be for kids who need glasses but cannot afford them.

Yash did research. He learned that more than 300 million people who need glasses cannot afford them. Yash also learned that millions of unwanted pairs of glasses get thrown away each year.

The teen came up with an idea to collect and donate the unwanted glasses. He started an organization called Sight Learning. Now Sight Learning provides glasses to students in need all around the world.

Increase your powers of empathy! Here are some ways:

1. Use your imagination. Practice understanding others' feelings by imagining you are a character in a book or movie. Think about what feelings you might have as that character.

2. Create an emotions poster. Cut out pictures from magazines that show people expressing different emotions. Write the matching emotion next to each picture.

3. Act it out. Play a game with friends where you act out a feeling without using words. See if they can guess what the feeling is.

Look at the photo. Can you guess what emotion this girl is acting out?

Read the story below and imagine what you might do in this situation.

Your friend falls during a soccer game and cuts her knee. She is really upset and hurt. How can you show empathy?

Need help getting started?

- Can you remember a time when you hurt yourself? How did you feel?

- Has someone ever made you feel better when you have gotten hurt? What did he or she do to help?

How Much Empathy Can You Show?

1. When a friend is sad, you:
    A. ask him or her to play a game.
    B. ignore him or her.
    C. ask him or her what is wrong.

2. Do friends come to you when they have a problem?
    A. Sometimes. I like to give advice.
    B. No, not too often.
    C. All the time.

3. If you see kids teasing someone, you:
    A. walk away.
    B. join the teasing.
    C. tell the other kids to stop.

Answer key: A: 2 points, B: 1 point, C: 3 points

If you scored 6–9 points, you are a very caring person! If you scored 3–5 points, try to start noticing the feelings of others more, as well as your own.

Glossary

emotion (ee-MOH-shun): strong feeling, such as happiness, sadness, or anger

empathy (EM-pah-thee): ability to share someone else's feelings

imagine (ih-MA-juhn): picture something in your mind

situations (sih-choo-WAY-shuns): things that affect people in a certain time and place

Index

Facts for Now

Visit this Scholastic Web site for more information on empathy:
www.factsfornow.scholastic.com
Enter the keyword **Empathy**

About the Author

Liz George is a writer and a licensed psychotherapist. She lives in Montclair, New Jersey, with her husband, Rob, her son, Zack, and her daughter, Ava. Liz enjoys helping teenagers get in touch with their feelings.